LOS ANGELES

ALSO BY JUDITH TAYLOR

Burning
Curios
Selected Dreams from the Animal Kingdom

SEX LIBRIS

JUDITH TAYLOR

WHAT
BOOKS
PRESS

LOS ANGELES

Copyright © 2013 by Judith Taylor. All rights reserved. Published in the United States by What Books Press, the imprint of the Glass Table Collective, Los Angeles.

Publisher's Cataloging-In-Publication Data
Taylor, Judith Nissman-
  Sex libris / Judith Taylor.
  p. ; cm.
  ISBN: 978-0-9889248-2-6
  1. Imagination--Poetry. 2. Dreams--Poetry. 3. Memory--Poetry. 4. American poetry--21st century. 5. Experimental poetry, American. I. Title.
PS3570.A94156 S49 2013
811/.54

What Books Press
10401 Venice Boulevard, no. 437
Los Angeles, California 90034

WHATBOOKSPRESS.COM

Cover art: Gronk, *Untitled*, 2012
Book design by Ashlee Goodwin, Fleuron Press
Author photo: Judith Taylor, *The Self and Others*

SEX LIBRIS

For Joan Nissman and Morton Abromson

CONTENTS

En Pointe, En Garde	13
Pink Velour Nightdress	14
Some Distant Songs	15
Night-Hag	16
Clinically Proven to Reduce	18
The Thinking Woman's Dust Mop	19
Private Eye	20
When Last She Gazed Out Her Casement Window	21
A Figure in the Toile	22
The Hiding Place of Goodbye	23
A Shadow, A Sonata	24
Small Poem	25
Writing in the Dark	26
For the Time Being	27
Coup de Théâtre	28
C'est Très Cher	29
Boo	30
Small House	32
Largo	33
The Well-Stocked Home	34
Munched on by Leaves	36
Tiny Book of Flying	37
Border	38
Floating World	40
Tossed into the Air	41

Bon Bon Perdu	42
In One Ear	43
Guidance is Internal	44
Sex Libris	45
Is	46
The Slippery Driveway	47
Grecian Yearn	48
Heart's Heat	49
Please Disarm the Opera	50
Lost Tales	51
The Encantatas	52
Camera Obscura	54
Flora and Fauna	55
Projects: Short List	56
My Blue Heaven	58
Secret Agent	59
Almost Audible	60
Stepford	61
Black Pot	62
Bone Encyclopedia	64
The Cards' Last Laugh	65
Acknowledgments	67
Notes	69

Yes, this is the dangerous, lucid hour. Who will knock at the door of my dressing-room, what face will come between me and the painted mentor peering at me from the other side of the looking-glass? Chance, my master and my friend, will, I feel sure, deign once more to send me the spirits of his unruly kingdom.

    Colette

EN POINTE, EN GARDE

I was either Giselle, wraithlike as well as mad,
or Miss Muffet, regurgitating after smashing the spider.

O whirling dervish memory!
O wedding-filigreed memory!

A dimple, a pill, a pearl, something
resembling a moonscape.

That time can whiteout experience, *tabula rasa* it —
well, it's astonishing, really.

I braid, I mend. I wave my magic wand
and turn a stallion into a sandwich.

There was a wedding, wasn't there, one bride, two
grooms, we inspected each other.

I had eyes in the back of my heart,
unflagging nails. My cashmeres changed

color with every humor. Ah, youth!
We can say Yes Father Yes or make a pledge

to clamber up the subversive. But more
Dads may follow, some sprouting two heads.

I hesitated and plunged at the same time.
It was never modest in that dance,

a language made out of pompoms, of granite.
Nothing I crave resembles anything I used to crave.

PINK VELOUR NIGHTDRESS

The one who is not The One appears in your sleep.

Fling away longings, those squirmy deep-sea creatures.

Does the cat follow you because you feed her or is she a haint?

By day you walk cool aisles buying anemones and fruit.

To work under the spell is not the same as working under the dream.

SOME DISTANT SONGS

Magpie, ragtag raga outside the window, what do you auger?

Birches creak in 4/4 time while deer drift across the field.

Don't try to remember. Doff the cloche of photographs.

Over time, the dreamer collects figures she calls "strangers."

Haunted by bits of memory, chiaroscuro of disturbing feathers.

NIGHT-HAG

It is a disease, which as one thinketh himselfe in the night to be oppressed with a great weight, and beleeveth that something cometh upon him.
  Method of Physick, 1664

Waking's lacy, frail and feathery.
If you combat bravely burnt toast,
grapefruit, you might matador yourself

into the day's tough hide. It can't be said
that I actually exist early mornings.

Then I'm my own aloof look-alike.
Sometimes, I don't abandon sleep
without a lingering slobbery goodbye

but sometimes sleep's been awful
and I don't want to date it ever again.

Long ago, some believed that if you
placed your shoes toes-out
underneath the bed, you'd ward off

Mera, night-hag who made
nightmares. Or hang a hag-stone

on the bedpost to deter the demon
from sitting on your chest, smothering
you while frightening you silly.

Beware too, the incubus who has his nasty
way with you while you snooze.

Medieval folk knew how dangerous
it is to close your lids. When my napping dogs
moaned and twitched, the vet said these

were happy canine moments — chasing cats
or rabbits—but in my opinion something

bad was harrying them. Last night, on
the dim repetitive stage of pale hours,
I craved not to be the star of my visions,

to be the understudy who never
goes on. Night moved through itself,

inexorably. Trees on shore like Chinese
cutouts, papery. No help, no help
this hypnogogic morning. On my chest

the night-hag squatted, pressing. It takes
longest to wake when you're broken.

CLINICALLY PROVEN TO REDUCE

Was it my knees or wits that gave out climbing Mt. McWhatever?

The adamantine of damage, running pure gold, deluxe.

Uneven, undone, unhinged: dream's hahahaha to the nerves.

You concoct a fanged mask but your neck's not intact.

A painted doll protected what was fine in me, cracked.

THE THINKING WOMAN'S DUST MOP

Look! My costume's blooming into an Acropolis of thought.

The explanation of a gavotte isn't quite sewn in yet.

Orbiting the room, I discover lost maps in the rafters.

Do I miss the translucence of a childhood full of paper?

Happenstance and extravagance meet, have sex, make syntax.

PRIVATE EYE

Follow the trail of clues.
If you know which are the clues.

>*gumshoe, shamus, flatfoot, sleuth*

If you were on a desert island
                    which death would you choose?

Loss: maelstrom, pushed to the teetery edge of plot.

The seeds: disappearance, theft, kidnapping, blackmail, murder.

The hero's ratiocination is the point. Beat up and battered, he'll recover in time for the next book. Warier, a tad more cynical, but game for the game.

The dick's flaws: drugs, drink, women.
Female dicks?   Men are the scar.

>*shadow, bloodhound, hawkshaw, tail*

Hungry lioness of crime.
Her twin? The need to hunt her down.

Reader, take comfort in the gospel of a cleansed world.

Hanging out in the lobby of your own mystery theater.

WHEN LAST SHE GAZED OUT HER CASEMENT WINDOW

Mind/Body   Body/Mind   Together?
Or, two entities — one essence and one thing?

Guess which one is the thing.

Sometimes she has been irritated with her thing.

Some days she is a poet wearing a pink bra.
Some days she *is* a pink bra.

Imprisoned in a tangled tower of words,
locks too short for a prince (!) to grab on to,
shorn on purpose. She supposes she's perverse.

No one's ever said the Mind/Body's logical.

Pop quiz: Describe one act/thought of a life's nano-moment.

She cooks, therefore she eats.
She eats, therefore (grumpily) she cooks.

Don't hate the body just because it's graspable.

Consciousness pulling the whole cartload along.
Sprightly pony.

A FIGURE IN THE TOILE

What do you have in mind? An ordinary roil in the hay?

I sense shambolic dust all over your choice of clothes.

An omen we're choosing to ignore our thresholds, our dogs.

Asleep, I dream the shaggy echo of chrysanthemums.

Unlock the notebook: torn hearts narrate on and on.

THE HIDING PLACE OF GOODBYE

Replication of mistakes: the thread of what might be called fate.

I escape from the fantastic, a warning or a sign of grace?

Dead leaves flood the floor when I open the door.

Don't look inside Pandora's Box of glamour then boredom.

When the fantasy fades, something worse could take its place.

A SHADOW, A SONATA

In a list of words one will always wink at you.

You can't undo your thought palace, that busy aerodrome.

My room circling volumes and the bones of a small love.

Can't we undo the teleology of boundaries?

Let it begin: the hunt for moonlight and susurration.

SMALL POEM

Heaviness like stone weighs down my eyes.

The horses' restlessness teams with my mood.

It's simply a hoot: the men with whom you dream sex.

The studs vie for the female; one is her mate, the king.

The temperature in between: not hot, not cold, waiting.

WRITING IN THE DARK

Fear's chandelier shakes the secluded house, TV sputters with its laugh track.

Our heroine must run from the house, its smoke-filled mirrors.

It is the formula as are her lovely yellow curls.

Why must she run out on the cliffs in pounding rain into the arms of the hero?

Hey, Goldie, don't flee to the sea, go into the woods.

Watch how the hills glisten before they darken to silhouette.

Now wait for the appearance of the wolf.

You should be prepared for his bony face.

There's a mask in your pocket, there always is.

Now you be the wolf.

FOR THE TIME BEING

The last time she saw him she couldn't push past the checkpoint.

She'll reinvent for you what she admired—that cummerbund
of confident ooze.

She was his itsy slice of bread, jelly on the side. (His belt has to fit!)

If she could trace her knotty path back into the forest, well, she simply
can't levitate enough these days to jump into those thickets, glutinous
as Mel Torme's croon.

In Nice or Monte Carlo, in Dubrovnik or Split, where the pink horizon
shivers with risk, a Martini is a mere fillip for what follows.

Where she quaffs, the sky's clearly a bore.

Oh, she's well bred, her dreams chiffony, her appetite lace. Watch her
muffle yawns with such politesse!

Who is she kidding? Her wish: waterlogged: to never extinguish
the bell, the slice, the wave.

COUP DE THÉÂTRE

The rain's svelte, subtle, gris: someone's gonna get soaked.

Equivocating ghosts loll on luxe-trimmed trees.

Emotions suddenly guillotined with habit's sardonic glee.

Getting wet's nothing but immersion—cleansing, ritualistic.

Toes and fingers gleam taupe, this season's to-die-for chic.

C'EST TRÈS CHER

Between snow and snow we slide into rumors and fences.

Trying to shoot photos that don't sing like postcards.

In my dream he's attached tiny stones to his billets-doux.

Am I caught again in the revolving door of cravings?

Living from one unremitting emporium to the next.

BOO

Sometimes I think the jet overhead
    Is a raging fly and sometimes I think

The nagging fly's a plane. Fragments of day
    And the ragged edgy night get mixed up

In the curly yellow batter of my head.
    The world's too svelte when squeezed, too

Miniature – it can pork out in front of your
    Dazed eyes. In the Galapagos Islands,

Birds don't fly away from humans,
    They preen and flap and mate quite happily

While we stand there, staring. I watched
    The Blue-footed Boobies' sex-samba.

Lucky. I love the deep chancey Black
    Lagoon from where what's possible

Lumbers out. Beginning's a cinch but
    No one really knows how things will end.

Incubus vision sucks out of us a tale
    We might not want to birth in the light of day.

All the ghost stories last night turned out
    To be jokes or fables. But I know of someone

Who ran out into the night because a dead child
   Suddenly loomed in his room.

Angel of the inexplicable or of madness?
   A hard winter's coming—the sky's

Blank white canvas, malevolent. Hi, bull
   I think of as intelligent because you swing around

Your huge domed head when I lope by,
   Do you know when the weather's going to attack

From above, but can't tell me? After I return
   Home the doctor wants to look carefully

At that mottled spot on my neck. I told her
   It was just my Galapagos tan peeling.

Months later, the cute little vampire mark
   Still clings to my untan skin. Reality

Comes up fast, like the hard vast earth
   When you're free falling and your chute

Won't open. Is some Thing here with me
   In this room? I hope what I'm hearing

Is my own jagged breath.

SMALL HOUSE

I stand at a window in a room with my love
watching the river

try to move out from under a blanket of ice

The Japanese have a word—*aware*—the moment of joy
infused with the sense of impermanence

Each moment containing its own epitaph

                where memory etches itself on delicate paper

LARGO

The dogs keep quiet.

The thumb doesn't throb.

When ennui spins gold, grab a spirit world to live in.

Half-breaths.
        Radiant doorway
        expectant.

Threshold before the mysteries let loose.

Not enough in it to hold the universe together?

Gravity's in a grave way.

Be careful
      not to push

            the
            down button
                    too hard.

Do I prefer story to the stifled light?

Porous music singing in my bearing heart.

White-dark night.

Oak tree.

THE WELL-STOCKED HOME

A complacent chair.

The old-fashioned four-poster bed of fate.

You should try to live in a town called Romance or Blue Eyes.

Wallpaper the kitchen with a charming pig and elephant motif.

Only at night are you allowed to open your Pandora's refrigerator.

Keep a large bunch of broccoli on hand to stun any alien being who might enter.

If a faucet drips, throw salt over both shoulders, it's faster than getting a plumber.

A large green bowl for memories.

A tiny chagrin box for forgetting.

If you're a liar, you'll need a winding staircase.

Oldish? Festoon yourself with birdcage earrings and a Stones tee.

A painting of three onions in varying stages of undress and tears.

Your mirror should be silver and a charmer.

A black safe in which to hide your fear of elevators.

A black safe in which to hide your fear of elevator men.

Re: the piano. Your children should play toccatas to settle down the toucans.

Are the books in your library dialectical, up to a point?

If a marauder enters, throw *Finnegans Wake* at him.

If that doesn't work, try Jonathan Franzen.

One window must be covered with Band-Aids.

For consolation, plant a weeping willow and poisonous mushrooms.

Speak politely to spiders, they produce such complicated jewelry.

A groping and kissing hallway.

A dining room table for oral sex.

If you live near a cornfield, don't ever bake pies.

Edge your house on dark forest, with an occluded path, but known to you.

Build a rumba room!

MUNCHED ON BY LEAVES

Pain rib-jazzes as the stations of night hours sift.

Your films looping direst dramas through you and through you.

Tint of mind-trick: the benign white flower on the tongue.

Will bones mend (a miracle!) for the doctors' cult?

Drip, drip: Time's faucet. I alone love you, says Percocet.

TINY BOOK OF FLYING

The wind keeps us alert on an island of threads.

Unread book open, not ripe yet for the feast.

Sleep: miraculous and rare like the Red Sea parting.

Pretty iffy the line between quirky and cracked.

My spirit guide mutters in Old Dutch: fate, fate.

BORDER

—Did you hate the rain *before* you were a wife?

—Do you underestimate the dialectical relationship between your heartaches, your toothaches, and the Republic of China?

—Can you do the arithmetic of your paltry desires in your head?

—We are x-raying your novel to analyze your instincts, which appear extinct to the naked eye.

—During the War Between the States, which side were your people on?

—We don't care if they were struggling to eat in a Russian shtetl, were they Yankee or Reb?

—Why won't your hair curl nicely without a cigarette? Or a cavalier?

—Given your history of fretting, what can you tell us about the history of the sundial?

—Do you think your sloppiness and your insomnia cut with the same knife?

—Are you avoiding plastic surgery merely because you've read Proust?

—What right do you think you have to your intuitions and why don't you like ducks?

—We are amazed at your ventriloquism. But who, dummy, is giving you those lines to mouth?

—When you look in the mirror does a beribboned sinking gondola come to mind?

—What nocturnal animal would you compare yourself to?

—Might your current tendency to pirouette without cease be the reason for your abrupt termination from the Alumni Society of your kindergarten?

—Why do you keep trying to delay your coronation?

—We've put you and your husband in separate rooms for questioning and can't help but notice that your answers, though equally hackneyed, are completely divergent.

—Do you wish to analyze why you refused your suitor that day at the lake?

—Was it the falling pinecones that gave you such disquietude?

FLOATING WORLD

Hello to the marimbas of mimicry and high-heels!

The blowsy décolletage of elegy I won't display.

Raise your perfumed umbrella. Cloudmood's such a slut.

Sip rock gut as the deer nibble blooms away.

Damages will be deducted from the bill of silence.

TOSSED INTO THE AIR

It's possible marriage flings candelabras against the void.

Also possible: marriage implodes into the Milky Way.

Shall we speculate upon what mansion and brothel have in common?

Nope, let's mutate. Enjoy our asanas, our cups of blankness.

The wine of error: how long it's taken to get the vintage just so.

BON BON PERDU

Once upon a time, longing choked me.

Don't be sad on this day of remembering and malls.

The cat's frozen water: tinny symphony of despair.

What we really know about light fills a very large sandwich.

I navigate blind and haunt beyond impulse's pale.

IN ONE EAR

Dregs float to the bottom of the cup.

Heat climbs onto your body, sticking like rape.

Brochures lure you to isles you'll never loll on.

New love, little wet whistle, witch watch trotting fast.

You press the shutter—presto!—the mirror vanishes.

GUIDANCE IS INTERNAL

a stage in the landing of space missiles

Just when it seemed her past was a pretty Klimt,
her lost cargo makes her a dishrag, a widow.

Rising and falling, her thoughts Braille into knots.
That fine mouth a window you can't open.

Should she be earnest or Javanese?
Toss her burning corsage into a ravine?

She'll show you the way to Cairo, but not to the kitchen.
It's simply ridiculous to be that small.

Ringaling! It's the chime for self-hypnosis.
She'd like to be alone now to cuddle her echo.

SEX LIBRIS

Where's language's little pointy bra?

Where's its waterfally bustier?

Imagination's crinoline, swish

of woosh? Who'll give one pence

for a mildewed thong? Fiction's hint:

fling yourself into something

foolish. New Material razz-

mattazzing with the ruddy body

of syntax. Emma B. says:

"The best amusement in the city

with a varied menu." ("Cheap

and sassy.") ("We like the waiters.")

Shall I coax the dog of sadness back?

Here boy, it's OK if you bite.

Words, I thought we were wedded for-

ever, rolling around on the shaggy

study rug. You've locked me out....

I hear books inside, righting themselves.

IS

I want to make clear
that it's a question of the curlicues
and the chandeliers. The rest
you can stash, slash, or cash. I'll
dissemble a toccata on the pianoforte
in the drawing room while you choose,
my Fata Morgana. The morgue
or the mosque of the impossibles.
Or is it the possibles? My near death
educated me: it's the same thing,
love. Fever Chandleresque,
a phalanx of similies breathing in me,
squeezing. Nothing solid anymore,
nada, zilch. How that patchwork itches!

Bring me my twilight Mai Tai
with your hoary paw, it's time
to read the old succulent
dramas tick-tocking on the mantel.
One can almost touch the fog
roiling in from the sea.
What's mysterious is how
persistent the brightness behind it
actually is.

THE SLIPPERY DRIVEWAY

The dial on the appliance is supposed to be turned on
to "sulk"
but she's twisting the setting to "rue."

It's the hour for her Blue Velvet cocktail.
That's a secret, dahling,
in whatever time zone chastisement lurks.

She worries that her eyebrows, and her chins,
are redundant.
Does this mean she is her own double,

or that her choicest parts are going out of warranty?
In either narrative,
her joists are hollow, it's hard to breathe

in the heaving ballroom. Nevertheless, it's better
to be bad-tempered
than to self-immolate, become food.

To the naked eye, she's opening a vein.
Whilst at the same time
she remains furtively fictive.

La la la. She trains these metallic chains,
her pretty things.
Whenever the moment strikes, she's right on time.

GRECIAN YEARN

The auto-da-fé sun devotes itself to our daylight faces.

I'd like to don cascading multi-braids like the frozen Kores.

Holding out my marble apples and doves to forever devotees.

I practice languid goddess makeup in my liquid boudoir.

Put on your "archaic smile," I whisper to no one, pleasantly noir.

HEART'S HEAT

The narcotic of utterance: it can cure or kill.

Such a simple, cunning word carried by a bird.

When truth is hushed, the frame will not contain it.

Do I have the courage to correctly read the signs?

The shivering of the maples: ominous or caress?

PLEASE DISARM THE OPERA

Leaning over history's balcony, looking down at the braided ribbons of chronology, one cheek tries to console the other, which cannot be consoled.

I am so afraid of heights.

"She was lonely. She kissed the clock."

Hand me a cigarette, I require rituals to cloak the mysteries.

How cool are the stretches of blessed myopia.
Shadowy, without newspapers, without light.

"Dangerous," she wrote, shivering, "Goya, Bosch."

If I open the forbidden box, what gestures would fly out!
If I were brave enough to be Tosca.

Laughingly: "Let's do the tango of sissies."

The fate of a persona? Skywriting, fading to whisper.

LOST TALES

The curtain's almost closed, the world's framed too narrow.

Instead of its wide wild rectangle, life's a thin bread slice.

Three elements: forest, field, rocks, smooth and cruel.

Insomnia's hollow sloppiness cuts into the journey.

Dwarves sleep in their coffins, what a poor tooth of a daughter.

Stories spin and spin, tangling golden locks into plots.

Father keeps shrinking and shrinking until he's gone.

The dark clot in your heart travels.

Oh child, you must invent new.

THE ENCANTATAS

> *We must however, acknowledge,...that man with*
> *his noble qualities,...still bears in his bodily frame*
> *the indelible stamp of his lowly origin.*
>   Charles Darwin

It's easy to mistake a Galapagos marine iguana
for lava, it having evolved such great protective
cover. The iguana and we are cousins—check it
out if you don't believe me—it's in the DNA.

Go too far with this, you turn boanthropic,
think you're an incarnated ox, and eat like one.
A few docs fought the smallpox vaccine,
thought if you were shot with cowpox,

you'd start to moo. Some of us all-day snackers
are secretly boanthropic. It's a disease that infects
writers. Go back farther, you find lycanthropes—
men who fancy themselves wolves.

Sure were a lot of those when I was a teen.
Darwin's bio reveals when he was young—
riding, shooting, carefree—no one thought
he was extraordinary. His Dad, a doctor,

taught him natural history. Many gentlemen,
and not a few ladies, amassed shells and fossils
the way we collect matches from the bountiful
shrinking globe. When Charles D., sailing

around Cape Horn on the Beagle, reached Galapagos,
the pushover placid birds perched as if posing
while they were shot for science. The oldest
island's only four million years old,

baby in time. Creatures came over gradually——
carried on driftwood, or they floated, flew,
were blown. Sea lion, turtle, booby, finch, flamingo,
albatross. An odd collection making the trip

to a new address. Some states teach evolution
alongside Creationism, God's plan: six days
of incredible effort on this bearded man's part,
then a day off feeling cocky. Every creature

stacked each on top of each, a neat hierarchy
with man alone at the top, Eve not quite up there.
Kids are supposed to choose: are you related
to God—or to a chimpanzee? Maybe

I've never been so at peace as when I sailed
around the Galapagos archipelago. Sea lions
stretched schnozzolas skyward catching rays,
the red-eyed swallow-tailed gull strutted inches

from us. All the animals laid-back, unafraid.
And squeamish me? I worked my way up
from small to massive iguanas, never freaked once.
Back home in LA, I almost shrieked when I saw

a huge yellow fellow, must have been three feet
counting his tail, laying across a woman's lap.
Iguanas are great pets, said she. *Hello! lady,
I saw him spit!* Some "relatives" you visit only

when they are the hosts.

CAMERA OBSCURA

The trail's almost obliterated, you ask him where is it.

You snap and snap as he walks away then back into the lens.

An orange dot, which the camera loses, though the eye keeps track.

You ask him to take a photo of you in the red scarf and hat.

You are not part of this landscape, the picture is a romance.

FLORA AND FAUNA

Hawk, surprised off his branch, circles twice, returns.

Beware the metaphor of the mirror, it will prove transitory.

You might minimize or exaggerate to prove the same theory.

Remember the garden belongs to darkness, not to be trusted.

Afternoon belongs to the deer, which stop, hearing Bach.

PROJECTS: SHORT LIST

Wear imagination's crinoline and its rustle puzzle.

Exhume from the grave your old chthonic songs.

Allow the corpse to dissent and smile this time.

Transform mind-nooses into louche earrings.

Paint Day-Glo numbers on the cloak-and-dagger clock.

Fight a tendency for a daisy petal approach to choice.

Plant dogs in fall so that spring will bark and frolic.

Abstract mist's perfume and wear it *sans* clothes.

Console when the air decides what will fail.

Sing the moon, its penny-wise, pound-foolish face.

Transform yourself into what Father and Mother dared not dream of.

Listen to Schumann mirror the long sinewy hours.

Compare day with high-button shoes, night with money.

Mock the hammer and praise the scissors.

Introduce charm to fidelity and hope they won't marry.

Dust and triage the splintered violet.

Praise the tasty sapphire salts of the body.

Replace one's own story with silk and bread.

Study the circles of history and its chains of desire.

Read all the books that sing subtly, riddling.

Drink when mood turns celadon and peals liquid.

Grieve when night's dusky shape is hunted down.

Listen for the swish swish: sound of attraction.

Memorize the seducer's motions, not his motives.

Wonder if you act out (poorly) your parent's secrets.

Celebrate each day's raised, plucked eyebrow.

Pray light will always canonize the window.

Die laughing on the black velvet Gothic chaise.

MY BLUE HEAVEN

When I came to, the pandemonium was worthless,
    a tiny shard of imbroglio.

The movie rolled, drooling its situations.
    I doused them all with sarcasm,
        a coda at the end of every doubt.

In the painting I'm splayed on the table,
in the painting I'm dancing in a cage,

vessel or vassal?

Too bad the order of things is bulletproof.

In the middle of every caress lies Tibet.
(Ditto for the spring song of the lindens.)

SECRET AGENT

He James Bonds us into giving up to him our secrets.

We're never sure we're as real as he.

The swift blue music of a double life.
The choreography of rules and anarchy.

One successful spy, an inside man, told me: Everyone, underneath, wishes to live slippery.

Our Man in Rio or DC kills coolly in the formal garden.

Shall we all walk through the mirror?
Kiss it, climb it, bind ourselves to it?

Reality won't reveal the name of the uberspy who mazes each smaller spy.
Nor reveal the ur-plot, the river that runs under all things.

Mint-on-pillow safe, do you love the boundary: suspense, then recovery?
Or, helpless, do you sing, *Murther, murther?*

None of us protected from our fates.

ALMOST AUDIBLE

When your picture fell out of the book, I felt nothing.

A portal to the past, transparent and forbidding.

Solitude's music, so quick to reappear, disappoint.

Put on the role, the carnival, soul's silver coffin.

Why be haunted by ghosts who have forgotten us?

STEPFORD

Sun lurks behind clouds unraveling like toilet paper.

Does my syntax translate to light and space, or vice versa?

Doll-wives kill real wives for the benefit of husbands.

This is old-fashioned weather: Zeus descends for his obliterations.

Ye gods mistake I'm a throwaway. I'm turned to stone.

BLACK POT

At dusk, the Blue Ridge sky's tinged
with the vague essence of wildness.

For us to sigh blissfully at the sight
of those distant heights, the Romantics

had to arrive hefting their lofty ideas
of the sublime. To some, forests,

those irreplaceable worlds of green
and shadow were "hideous."

Satan and his ilk hung out there. Peasants
Said to daughters: Don't go in! Do you want

to be tupped by the devil? OK, don't
answer! Our Salem Witches did Sabbaths

in the woods. The Big Bad Wolf lurks,
the old crone's home of hot sweets squats.

Unless you run fast you will be one sad cookie.
What happens in the forest alters your view

big time of the transparent world.
Or you don't come out. Well, this is old belief.

Now we're cool about the Other denuded
of mystery. What does November taste like?

You say pumpkin, I say smoke. You say
turkey, I say fishes of the air. Not pilgrims,

but the tattered scraps of the Immortals.
Turn the corner of morning, catch the blazing

fox trotting out of the forest. Tumble down
cellar steps, suck out the unaccountable

remnants from midnight's larder. Abandon
lanterns, sense the disobedient borders

of the ordinary. Witches with their phallic
broomsticks were the bad girls of yesteryear,

the ones with guts, the untrammeled.
And while we're on the subject, what happened

to a certain witch's wayward nature?
One day she woke, shorn of her wild

turbulent mane. Nearby, mountains ride
the air, stands of ancient oaks remain.

Every thing of the earth's aging, too,
but slowly, slowly. How easy it is now

for her to be tame. It has nothing to do
with goodness.

BONE ENCYCLOPEDIA

So strange to go naked without pretty earrings.

In the thick evening silence, blue moth wings.

I won't conjure up the decorative frills of avoidance.

I think in time we are all simple beings.

When a tree is shorn, see what lives in the limbs.

THE CARDS' LAST LAUGH

The doll's dilemma: should she be lyric or play the sax?

If you wander, there will be a sequel, not an exit.

Shall we solve the riddle of fossils and decorative clothes?

Ship ahoy! The wind's insistence that you walk across the bridge.

It doesn't matter if you button up, it always comes undone.

ACKNOWLEDGMENTS

Grateful acknowledgment to the editors of the following publications in which these poems first appeared, sometimes in different versions.

5AM "Night-Hag"

Antioch Review "For the Time Being"

Catch Up "Clinically Proven to Reduce"

Columbia Poetry Review "Floating World"

Conduit "Private Eye"

Court Green "Grecian Yearn," "Stepford," "When Last She Gazed Out Her Casement Window"

Dragonfire "Black Pot," "Border"

Field "Sex Libris"

Fifth Wednesday "Bone Encyclopedia," "The Thinking Woman's Dust Mop"

Gulf Coast "Boo"

Parthenon West "My Blue Heaven," "Please Disarm the Opera," "Secret Agent"

Pleiades "Largo"

Prairie Schooner "The Encantatas"

Slope "A Figure in the Toile," "Flora and Fauna," "Pink Velour Nightdress," "The Cards' Last Laugh"

The Writing Disorder "Almost Audible," "A Shadow, A Sonata," "Bon Bon Perdu," "Coup de Théâtre," "In One Ear," "Is," "Munched on by Leaves," "Some Distant Songs," "The Hiding Place of Goodbye"

Van Gogh's Ear "Small House"

The Los Angeles Poetry Review "Lost Tales," "Writing in the Dark"

VOLT "En Pointe, En Garde"

My gratitude to the Corporation of Yaddo, the Ucross Foundation Residency Program, and the Virginia Center for the Creative Arts for their generous support while I was writing these poems.

Janet Kaplan's enthusiastic and insightful reading of this manuscript benefited it enormously.

My appreciation to Gail Wronsky, Chuck Rosenthal, Karen Kevorkian, and the folks at What Books.

NOTES

The book's epigraph is from Colette's novel, *The Vagabond*.

"Pink Velour Nightdress" The last line is from Louise Bourgeois's writings.

"My Blue Heaven" is dedicated to Cathy Colman.

"Private Eye" The names in italics are nicknames for private eyes, some not in general use anymore.

"Coup de Théâtre" is a French term meaning a sudden dramatic turn of events in a play or an unexpected sensational event that reverses a situation.

"Tiny Book of Flying" is dedicated to 'Annah Sobelman.

"Grecian Yearn" Kores are large stone sculptures of female figures from the Greek Archaic Period. Huge ones found near the Parthenon can now be seen in the Acropolis Museum, Athens. Their faces are said to express "archaic smiles."

"The Encantatas" is dedicated to Candace Falk.

"Stepford" I'm thinking of the 1975 *The Stepford Wives* film, now a camp feminist classic, not the lackluster 2004 remake. Both films were based on the 1972 novel by Ira Levin.

JUDITH TAYLOR is the author of two previous poetry collections, *Curios* and *Selected Dreams from the Animal Kingdom*, and a chapbook, *Burning*. She's the co-editor of *Air Fare: Stories, Poems and Essays on Flying*. Her work has been included in numerous anthologies and journals. She is the recipient of a Pushcart Prize. Currently, she teaches private classes, travels, takes photographs, and co-edits the online poetry journal *POOL*. judithtaylorpoet.com

TITLES FROM
WHAT BOOKS PRESS

POETRY

Molly Bendall & Gail Wronsky, *Bling & Fringe (The L.A. Poems)*
Kevin Cantwell, *One of Those Russian Novels*
Ramón García, *Other Countries*
Karen Kevorkian, *Lizard Dream*
Chuck Rosenthal, Gail Wronsky, Gronk, *Tomorrow You'll Be One of Us: Sci Fi Poems*
Judith Taylor, *Sex Libris*
Lynne Thompson, *Start with a Small Guitar*
Gail Wronsky, *So Quick Bright Things*, bilingual, Spanish, tr. Alicia Partnoy

FICTION

François Camoin, *April, May, and So On*
A.W. DeAnnuntis, *Master Siger's Dream*
A.W. DeAnnuntis, *The Mermaid at the Americana Arms Motel*
Katharine Haake, *The Origin of Stars and Other Stories*
Katharine Haake, *The Time of Quarantine*
Mona Houghton, *Frottage & Even As We Speak: Two Novellas*
Rod Val Moore, *Brittle Star*
Chuck Rosenthal, *Coyote O'Donohughe's History of Texas*

MAGIC JOURNALISM

Chuck Rosenthal, *Are We Not There Yet? Travels in Nepal, North India, and Bhutan*
Chuck Rosenthal, *West of Eden: A Life in 21st Century Los Angeles*

ART

Gronk, *A Giant Claw*, bilingual intro, Spanish
Chuck Rosenthal, Gail Wronsky, Gronk, *Tomorrow You'll Be One of Us: Sci Fi Poems*

LOS ANGELES

What Books Press books may be ordered from:
SPDBOOKS.ORG | ORDERS@SPDBOOKS.ORG | (800) 869 7553 | AMAZON.COM

Visit our website at
WHATBOOKSPRESS.COM

CPSIA information can be obtained at www.ICGtesting.com
Printed in the USA
LVOW06s0128040913

350749LV00003B/5/P